THE JOURNEY CONTINUES VOL. 2

CUT DOWN BUT NOT ABANDONED

WILLIAM HATFIELD

ACKNOWLEDGEMENTS

We are all on a journey through life! I want to thank all my family and friends who stand besides me and encourage me when times are tough.

I especially want to thank my aunt Viola for all her work in editing and preparing the manuscript of my first book for publishing. The knowledge she shared will help me to continue writing.

TABLE OF CONTEXT

DEDICATION

I dedicate this book to the thirsty and hungry saints of God that desire an intimacy with the Holy Spirit like no other. My prayer is that you can find this journey as a source of encouragement, strength and power to overcome life's struggles and walk in a greater sense of freedom and relationship with the Holy Spirit and all within your sphere of influence.

PROLOGUE

This book is about the journey of a young man called into the five-fold ministry. Being introduced to Jesus as a 6 year old was exciting, but growing in your relationship with Jesus is not what I thought it might be. My love for Jesus was never in question as I began to grow in hearing the multitude ways that the Holy Spirit communicates with his creation. This is the journey of a young man discovering relationship with the Holy Spirit verses religion of church. We are all on a journey that will continue on into eternity. Everybody's journey is different so let's have grace and love for each other and except that fact that God never created cookie cutter Christians. By sharing our individual journeys with each other we can come into the revelation knowledge of the goodness of

God in our lives.

We all have past history that is best left in the past.

Philippians 3:13-14King James Version (KJV)

13 Brethren, I count not myself to have
apprehended: but this one thing I do,
forgetting those things which are behind,
and reaching forth unto those things
which are before,

14 I press toward the mark for the prize of
the high calling of God in Christ Jesus.

A LESSON FROM THE PAST

As I sit and begin to put this book together I pray Holy Spirit help me, give me a good opening. He responded write your heart. So this book is about my perspective of the Christian life. The ups and downs, good times and not so good times. The times when you act out in zealousness only to be shot down. The times when you hear from God and are excited only to have good Christian folk ask are you sure that's not the devil?

In this end time…correction, the end times started over 2000 years ago on the day of Pentecost. We are in the last days. My journey started at the age of six about 1971 at a Pentecostal bible camp where I accepted Jesus as savior. Everything was great for the next four years. We lived in Grovedale on a farm. As children we were not sheltered or coddled. We were taught to work and work hard. My stepfather was of German descent and at the age of 45 he found himself married to my mother with seven children. I don't know off hand any bible verse that says have children in your youth or younger years; but from experience I found it easier to raise children when you have as much energy as them. Sorry as I am researching and typing I found one 1 Timothy 5:14 **I will therefore that the younger women marry, bear children, and guide the house…**

My stepfather did have one fall back that may have hampered his ability to raise children just a little bit. He loved his beer. I remember one time my sister Janet was washing dishes and she was almost finished when our stepfather checked the dish water and got mad because it was getting cold and greasy from the dishes. He hollered at her because she never changed the water earlier and then grabbed her by the head and pushed her head under the water. That was her way of reminding her to change the dish water regularly to have hot clean water to get dishes clean. Sad to say it wasn't long before my sister left home and went to live with one of my relatives on Vancouver Island. Our stepfather's way of discipline was very simple. If the culprit didn't own up to their mischievous deed then every child got a beating with a six inch wide one inch thick conveyor belt.

After a few years when I was long gone from home and had a son of my own I visited him. I told him we really never liked how he raised us but I was very grateful to him because he taught me how to work. I talked to him about Jesus and he told me that he grew up as catholic and was even an altar boy. He did accept Jesus as his savior but never had any teaching and lived carnally all his life. Most, if not all, people don't have a revelation of how far the grace, mercy and love of God goes. When my mother was on her death bed she would slip in and out of a comma. When she was in the comma she would talk with Jesus and He would give her messages for her children and her current husband. In one of the commas she said that our stepfather was with Jesus and told her to hurry up so they could go dancing. I believed her because years earlier a group of us were in intercessory prayer for the lost and when we prayed for our stepfather the Holy Spirit gave one of the intercessors a vision. The vision was of a wall of mailboxes in heaven and our stepfather's name Harry Servatius was on it. There is a saying I heard a few years ago that goes, "When you get to Heaven you will be surprised who's there and who isn't." I believe this with all my heart. Many deathbed decisions have been made crying out to Jesus with their last breath.

Romans 10:13 King James Bible
for whosoever shall call upon the name of the Lord shall be saved.

One of the thieves beside Jesus on the cross is a prime example.

Anyways, just giving you some background information, I never had a Godly upbringing just a moral one. The Baptist church was a few miles from our farm and the pastor showed up one day and asked my mother if He could pick us up in the bus and take us to Sunday school. My mother agreed.

As a young child I never really understood a lot of what I was taught about Jesus. One thing that I knew for sure though was that Jesus loved us and would never hurt us. Attending the country Baptist church was the highlight of my week I really enjoyed church, hearing the stories, making crafts, and meeting new people. The day seemed like any other day in a long endless succession of days filled with chores and playtime. That evening was like any other evening, suppertime, homework, a little television and then off to bed.

As I put my head to the pillow I remembered to pray. During church I remember hearing about a devil that liked to hurt people but also heard how to make him go away as well. I couldn't quite remember the word my cousin told me to use so I would say, 'devil I refugee you in the Name of Jesus, you stay away from my family." It wasn't until a few years later that I realized the word was rebuke rather than refugee; but to a little child it did not matter what the word was as long as the devil stayed away.

Unknown to me the Holy Spirit was planning a supernatural visitation as soon as the household had retired for the night.

Well into the early hours of the morning a light illuminating the interior of our house awakened me. Something was drawing me to the source of the light. As I walked into the kitchen I realized the light started outside radiating in. I was compelled into the porch and outside to the steps. The most marvelous sight I had ever seen appeared in the sky above me. A large pair of hands appeared in the sky held together in prayer. The hands began to open and a bible appeared. This bible was so huge it seemed to fill the entire sky. I stood in awe as a passage of scripture was circled.

The scripture was Ezekiel 3:10-11, "Moreover He said to me: "Son of man, receive into your heart all my words that I speak to you, and hear with your ears. And go, get to the captives, to the children of your people, and speak to them and tell them, 'Thus says the Lord God,' whether they hear, or whether they refuse."

After a minute or so of watching this scene I was translated to the far end of my stepfather's grain field. My brothers and sisters were with me. We were standing beside the flat top hay wagon when Jesus appeared. He was wearing royal purple robes and radiated the most brilliant light I had ever seen. The glory radiating from Christ was so brilliant that creation ceased to exist, all you could see was Jesus and His glory, and nothing else was visible.

Jesus stood before us, His hand extended to us. In His hand was a piece of fruit of some sort. He presented this fruit to us, we all stood staring not sure what to do. I took the fruit from His hand and stood in amazement looking at this fruit, as it was not like anything we had ever seen. I decided to take a bite of the fruit. As soon as I bit off a piece of the fruit, the vision ended, I was sitting on the edge of my bed, daylight pouring in through the windows, wondering about the events that just took place.

I never really understood that vision as a child, but one thing was very clear to me; from that time on I wanted to be a minister of the Gospel of Jesus Christ.

I tried to share that Vision and desire to be a minister with family but my family never seemed to understand what was going on in my life. My mother just watched me grow in my desire for God. A few years later on her deathbed she told me of a time when she found me running around in the house with a bible in my hand. She asked me what I was doing and I told her I was chasing after God. She then told me I couldn't catch God and that I was to sit still and let Him catch me. One church meeting stood out strong in my mind since it was probably one of the last meetings I attended as a child. A young girl sang a special song in which I found great pleasure. I started clapping wanting to show appreciation for the beautiful song she sung. The Pastor chewed me out severely in front of the congregation; he then proceeded to smack my hands with a pointer stick for not having respect for the things of God. I never could figure out how clapping showed disrespect for God. This form of rejection convinced me to stay away from church and anything to do with God.

If you read my first two books you are familiar with some of the visions and dreams shared in this book. They are worth repeating because of the theme of the book. How did this affect you? Well it planted a religious seed in my life which affects my attitude in church. For example the worship leader finishes their set with, "Let's give Jesus a clap offering for what He is going to do." The congregation claps and cheers like a Christian pop star comes on the stage. I get a little disturbed inside and one day I thought let's just applaud Jesus our rock star for performing for us. I never realized my thoughts were verbal and loud enough for a few people around me to hear. I looked around thinking I might have offended them but they were not acting like the rest of the congregation.

The Pastor comes to the stage calls the children up, prays a blessing over them and releases them to their classes. The pastor preaches a message that may or may not be a blessing or encouragement to the congregation. This goes on week after week and no obvious manifestation of the Holy Spirit. You think well maybe someone will get up and testify of the goodness of God in their lives. Nothing is said so we repeat this performance week after week. Where's God! Why didn't He perform some mighty acts like we applauded and clapped our hands until they hurt?

Are we missing something? Maybe we should have a whole two hour service where we just clap and applaud Jesus for what He is about to do. I looked for scripture that tells men to clap for Jesus and this is one that came up on google search.

Psalm 98:5-9 5Sing unto the LORD with
the harp; with the harp, and the voice of
a psalm. 6With trumpets and sound of
cornet make a joyful noise before the
LORD, the King. 7Let the sea roar, and
the fullness thereof; the world, and they
that dwell therein. 8Let the floods clap
their hands: let the hills be joyful together
9Before the LORD; for he cometh to judge
the earth: with righteousness shall he
judge the world, and the people with

This comment was found dealing with the verse. The Bible says in Psalm 98:8 that the rivers (or the oceans, depending on your Bible version) clap their hands to praise God. So why shouldn't Christians do the same? I mean, we human beings actually have literal hands, so we should be a leg up (and a hand up) on those rivers and oceans that only have metaphorical hands to praise with!

Not satisfied with that explanation of that verse I decided to meditate about when God moved in my life or in a church service I was in. I was walking from the south side of Grande Prairie where I lived, I got to the IGA parking lot and I heard deep in my spirit, "WORSHIP ME." I dropped right there on the grass beside the sidewalk and put my face in the lawn and stretched out my arms above my head and began to worship God. I did this until an overwhelming peace consumed me. And no I wasn't concerned about the people walking by. I was engrossed and consumed with worshipping my one and only true Father in heaven. I had a great day that day. Any adventure that confronted me I easily overcame and put my head down that night in total peace.

Another time I went to a meeting in Hythe. The praise and worship was great people raised their hands and were swaying back and forth. I felt impressed to drop to my knees and then to my belly with my face in the floor, arms stretched over my head and began to worship. After about ten minutes I got back to my knees and noticed people all over the congregation were on their knees worshipping God. Some had their arms reaching heaven while others had their hands folded in prayer on their chest. The atmosphere was one of reverence and worship for who God is rather than what He can or would do. The guest speaker got off his knees and began ministering to that farming community concerning issues they were facing. The revelation gifts began to move through the speaker and myself and others. God ministered to His people concerning their situations and the people left joyful knowing God showed up and was helping them with their lives.

The bible says in 1 Timothy 2:8 King James Bible
I will therefore that men pray everywhere, lifting up holy hands, without wrath and doubting.

Psalm 63:4
so I will bless you as long as I live; I will lift up my hands in your name.

Psalm 134:2
Lift up your hands to the sanctuary and bless the LORD.

Nehemiah 8:6 King James Bible
And Ezra blessed the LORD, the great God. And all the people answered, Amen, Amen, with lifting up their hands: and they bowed their heads, and worshipped the LORD with *their* faces to the ground.

2 Chronicles 7:3 King James Bible
And when all the children of Israel saw how the fire came down, and the glory of the LORD upon the house, they bowed themselves with their faces to the ground upon the pavement, and worshipped, and praised the LORD, *saying*, For *he is* good; for his mercy *endureth* for ever.

I have found many scriptures on lifting hands and being on your face before God. I haven't come across clapping your hands, just the interpretation of one person on Psalm 98:8. I am not going to be dogmatic about it but the proof is in the eating of the pudding. When I am on my face before God and raise my hands in worship for which He is then the Holy Spirit manifests. When I clap for what He is about to do I experience the routine of men? One is in faith and the other is doubt. I worship him because of the finished work at the cross and I am not expecting Him to do what has already been done.

2 Peter 1:3 King James Bible
According as his divine power hath given unto us all things that *pertain* unto life and godliness, through the knowledge of him that hath called us to glory and virtue:

The clapping puts Jesus in the same category as men. We show appreciation to men when they please us with a great performance. We make Jesus common as man by doing to Him what we would do to a man who pleases us or inspires us. I think making Jesus common like any man shows disrespect and bordering on blasphemy. I think this scripture fits clapping

2 Timothy 3:5King James Version (KJV)

5 Having a form of godliness, but denying the power thereof: from such turn away.

I am not here to judge people. If you want to clap go right ahead but as for me I like raising my hands and being on my face before God. I have a close intimate relationship with my Heavenly Father because of it. I won't trade that for all the applause in the world. You know that pastor slapping my hands with the pointer stick actually unknowingly planted a God seed in me. I was clapping for the person singing not God but his legalistic thinking couldn't let him go beyond that. I have been to church many times over the years and one thing I am tired of and that's meeting man every time I darken the door of a church. I want to meet God and experience the precious Holy Spirit in manifestation.

GOD IN THE HIGHEST

Praise be to God from whom all blessings flow
With love and worship, to Him I shall go
He is my fortress and strong tower
My Jesus comes with resurrection power

He is the light and joy of life
Keeping me from harm and all strife

He is my soon coming King
Bringing joy and causing all to sing

He is the one who looks to my best
Giving joy, peace and eternal rest
Of all the things that come my way
I'll look forward to resurrection day.

SNOWFLAKE CHRISTIANS

Christianity today..........would the apostles of the book of acts recognize it as the same good news they gave their lives to promote? When John penned the book of Revelation he received messages for the seven churches of Asia Minor. These messages not only proved to apply to the current situation but also seemed to show the historical progression of the church.

Revelation 2-3 KJV

Chapter 2

THE LOVELESS CHURCH

1 Unto the angel of the church of Ephesus write; these things saith he that holdeth the seven stars in his right hand, who walketh in the midst of the seven golden candlesticks;

2 I know thy works, and thy labour, and
thy patience, and how thou canst not
bear them which are evil: and thou hast
tried them which say they are apostles,
and are not, and hast found them liars:
3 And hast borne, and hast patience, and
for my name's sake hast laboured, and
hast not fainted.
4 Nevertheless I have somewhat against
thee, because thou hast left thy first love.
5 Remember therefore from whence thou
art fallen, and repent, and do the first
works; or else I will come unto thee
quickly, and will remove thy candlestick
out of his place, except thou repent.
6 But this thou hast, that thou hatest the
deeds of the Nicolaitans, which I also
hate.
7 He that hath an ear let him hear what
the Spirit saith unto the churches; to him
that overcometh will I give to eat of the
tree of life, which is in the midst of the
paradise of God.

THE PERSECUTED CHURCH
8 And unto the angel of the church in
Smyrna write; these things saith the first
and the last, which was dead, and is
alive;
9 I know thy works, and tribulation, and
poverty, (but thou art rich) and I know
the blasphemy of them which say they
are Jews, and are not, but are the
synagogue of Satan.
10 Fear none of those things which thou
shalt suffer: behold, the devil shall cast
some of you into prison, that ye may be
tried; and ye shall have tribulation ten
days: be thou faithful unto death, and I
will give thee a crown of life.
11 He that hath an ear let him hear what
the Spirit saith unto the churches; He that
overcometh shall not be hurt of the
second death.
THE COMPROMISING CHURCH

12 And to the angel of the church in
Pergamos write; these things saith he
which hath the sharp sword with two
edges;
13 I know thy works, and where thou
dwellest, even where Satan's seat is: and
thou holdest fast my name, and hast not
denied my faith, even in those days
wherein Antipas was my faithful martyr,
who was slain among you, where Satan
dwelleth.
14 But I have a few things against thee,
because thou hast there them that hold
the doctrine of Balaam, who taught Balac
to cast a stumbling block before the
children of Israel, to eat things sacrificed
unto idols, and to commit fornication.
15 So hast thou also them that hold the
doctrine of the Nicolaitans, which thing I
hate.
16 Repent; or else I will come unto thee
quickly, and will fight against them with
the sword of my mouth.

17 He that hath an ear, let him hear what
the Spirit saith unto the churches; to him
that overcometh will I give to eat of the
hidden manna, and will give him a white
stone, and in the stone a new name
written, which no man knoweth saving
he that receiveth it.

THE CORRUPT CHURCH

18 And unto the angel of the church in
Thyatira write; these things saith the Son
of God, who hath his eyes like unto a
flame of fire, and his feet are like fine
brass;
19 I know thy works, and charity, and
service, and faith, and thy patience, and
thy works; and the last to be more than
the first.
20 Notwithstanding I have a few things
against thee, because thou sufferest that
woman Jezebel, which calleth herself a

prophetess, to teach and to seduce my
servants to commit fornication, and to eat
things sacrificed unto idols.
21 And I gave her space to repent of her
fornication; and she repented not.
22 Behold, I will cast her into a bed, and
them that commit adultery with her into
great tribulation, except they repent of
their deeds.
23 And I will kill her children with death;
and all the churches shall know that I am
he which searcheth the reins and hearts:
and I will give unto every one of you
according to your works.
24 But unto you I say, and unto the rest
in Thyatira, as many as have not this
doctrine, and which have not known the
depths of Satan, as they speak; I will put
upon you none other burden.
25 But that which ye have already hold
fast till I come.

26 And he that overcometh, and keepeth
my works unto the end, to him will I give
power over the nations:
27 And he shall rule them with a rod of
iron; as the vessels of a potter shall they
be broken to shivers: even as I received of
my Father.
28 And I will give him the morning star.
29 He that hath an ear let him hear what
the Spirit saith unto the churches.

Chapter 3

THE DEAD CHURCH

1 And unto the angel of the church in
Sardis write; These things saith he that
hath the seven Spirits of God, and the
seven stars; I know thy works, that thou
hast a name that thou livest, and art
dead.
2 Be watchful, and strengthen the things
which remain, that are ready to die: for I
have not found thy works perfect before
God.

3 Remember therefore how thou hast
received and heard, and hold fast, and
repent. If therefore thou shalt not watch, I
will come on thee as a thief, and thou
shalt not know what hour I will come
upon thee.
4 Thou hast a few names even in Sardis
which have not defiled their garments;
and they shall walk with me in white: for
they are worthy.
5 He that overcometh, the same shall be
clothed in white raiment; and I will not
blot out his name out of the book of life,
but I will confess his name before my
Father, and before his angels.
6 He that hath an ear let him hear what
the Spirit saith unto the churches.

THE FAITHFUL CHURCH

7 And to the angel of the church in
Philadelphia write; These things saith he
that is holy, he that is true, he that hath
the key of David, he that openeth, and no
man shutteth; and shutteth, and no man
openeth;
8 I know thy works: behold, I have set
before thee an open door, and no man
can shut it: for thou hast a little strength,
and hast kept my word, and hast not
denied my name.
9 Behold, I will make them of the
synagogue of Satan, which say they are
Jews, and are not, but do lie; behold, I
will make them to come and worship
before thy feet, and to know that I have
loved thee.
10 Because thou hast kept the word of
my patience, I also will keep thee from
the hour of temptation, which shall come
upon all the world, to try them that dwell
upon the earth.

11 Behold, I come quickly: hold that fast
which thou hast, that no man takes thy
crown.
12 Him that overcometh will I make a
pillar in the temple of my God, and he
shall go no more out: and I will write
upon him the name of my God, and the
name of the city of my God, *which is* new
Jerusalem, which cometh down out of
heaven from my God: and *I will write*
upon him my new name.
13 He that hath an ear let him hear what
the Spirit saith unto the churches.

THE LUKE WARM CHURCH

14 And unto the angel of the church of
the Laodiceans write; these things saith
the Amen, the faithful and true witness,
the beginning of the creation of God;
15 I know thy works, that thou art neither
cold nor hot: I would thou wert cold or
hot.
16 So then because thou art lukewarm,
and neither cold nor hot, I will spue thee
out of my mouth.

17 Because thou sayest, I am rich, and
increased with goods, and have need of
nothing; and knowest not that thou art
wretched, and miserable, and poor, and
blind, and naked:
18 I counsel thee to buy of me gold tried
in the fire, that thou mayest be rich; and
white raiment, that thou mayest be
clothed, and *that* the shame of thy
nakedness do not appear; and anoint
thine eyes with eye salve, that thou
mayest see.
19 As many as I love, I rebuke and
chasten: be zealous therefore, and repent.
20 Behold, I stand at the door, and knock:
if any man hears my voice, and opens the
door, I will come in to him, and will sup
with him, and he with me.
21 To him that overcometh will I grant to
sit with me in my throne, even as I also
overcame, and am set down with my
Father in his throne?

22 He that hath an ear let him hear what the Spirit saith unto the churches.

I believe we are living in the Laodicea era. I say that based on a leadership meeting I was in where the pastor commented, we believe in the Holy Spirit but we will not preach on it. Calling the Holy Spirit it shows you don't know who He is. The manifestations of the Holy Spirit are not welcome so there is no manifestation. This church is heavy on classes to gain knowledge and giving certificates to people who took these classes. But while they are getting knowledge sin abounds in the church. They get to brag about the framed paper they have on their walls. Their great classes and courses give them standing with other churches in their denomination.

Another church I attended and took their membership class presented the prospective members with a document called covenant. This document stated that you would tithe to the church but no where's was anything saying what the church would do for you. A covenant is a two Way Street, not a statement that basically says you should be honored to be a part of our organization and will give money. We don't have to have responsibility to and for you. In my mind this is empire building and not kingdom building.

The church thought of itself as rich and in need of nothing from Christ. Although many of the members may have been materially rich, the "wealth" it claimed for it would be spiritual. What is in view here is Laodicea's spiritual pride and complacency .I believe we are living in the Laodicea church age. There are mega churches that are seeker friendly with great music, charismatic speakers and receive large offerings. These mega churches think that their size and affluence make them great in God's eyes.

One denominational church I was in for a couple of years made it quite clear in a leadership meeting; we believe in the Holy Spirit but we won't preach or teach on it.

2 Corinthians 4:13 King James Bible We having the same spirit of faith, according as it is written, I believed, and therefore have I spoken; we also believe, and therefore speak;

For a pastor to say I believe but I won't preach on what I believe especially the Holy Spirit is robbing his congregation. The Holy Spirit is God and since the day of Pentecost when the Holy Spirit came to the earth we are living in His time. The Holy Spirit is the most valued and honored of the God Head.

Matthew 12:32 King James Bible

And whosoever speaketh a word against the Son of man, it shall be forgiven him: but whosoever speaketh against the Holy Ghost, it shall not be forgiven him, neither in this world, neither in the *world* to come.

To not allow the Holy Spirit and His manifestations in your church you allow an evil spirit of religion in your church. You can tell when religion is at work when you challenge their belief system. Religious people will get mad and justify themselves. They will try to put you down. We had a short discussion of the Holy Spirit manifestation of tongues and a religious man who is a leader in this denominational church attacked me by saying; "you received the Holy Spirit and power (Acts 1:8) well where's your power?" He was very angry when he confronted us and I knew better to respond because he was in no place to hear me.

I believe denominational churches that don't allow the Holy Spirit to have placed in their church are the church of Sardis. Revelation 3:1…they have a reputation amongst their denomination because of the great works they do but in God's eyes they are dead. Why? Because the works they do are works of the flesh and they receive stature among men. To allow the Holy Spirit to manifest through you takes you out of the equation and allows God to get the credit and the praise and the honor.

Galatians 5:16-26 King James Version
16 This I say then, Walk in the Spirit, and ye shall not fulfil the lust of the flesh.

17 For the flesh lusteth against the Spirit, and the Spirit against the flesh: and these are contrary the one to the other: so that ye cannot do the things that ye would.

18 But if ye be led of the Spirit, ye are not under the law.

19 Now the works of the flesh are
manifest, which are these; Adultery,
fornication, uncleanness, lasciviousness,

20 Idolatry, witchcraft, hatred, variance,
emulations, wrath, strife, seditions,
heresies,

21 Envyings, murders, drunkenness,
revellings, and such like: of which I tell
you before, as I have also told you in time
past, that they which do such things shall
not inherit the kingdom of God.

22 But the fruit of the Spirit is love, joy,
peace, longsuffering, gentleness,
goodness, faith,

23 Meekness, temperance: against such
there is no law.

24 And they that are Christ's have
crucified the flesh with the affections and
lusts.

25 If we live in the Spirit, let us also walk
in the Spirit.

26 Let us not be desirous of vain glory,
provoking one another, envying one
another

The snowflake Christian is one who desires glory from men which is vain. They admire their reputation and provoke others to get what they have. By not having the Spirit of God manifest in their lives they open themselves up to other strange spirits. The answer for snowflake Christianity is to

REPENT and seek after the Holy Spirit.

2 Corinthians 13:14 New American Standard Bible
The grace of the Lord Jesus Christ, and the love of God, and the fellowship of the Holy Spirit, be with you all.

King James Bible
The grace of the Lord Jesus Christ, and the love of God, and the communion of the Holy Ghost, *be* with you all. Amen.

VALUE

The funny thing about value is....WHERE WE LOOK TO GET IT.

val·ue

[ˈvalyo͞o]

VERB

Values (third person present)

1. estimate the monetary worth of (something):

"His estate was valued at $45,000"

Synonyms: evaluate · assess · estimate · appraise · price ·

2. consider (someone or something) to be important or beneficial; have a high opinion of:

"She had come to value her privacy and independence"

Synonyms: think highly of · have a high opinion of ·

Hold in high regard ·rate highly ·esteem ·set (great) store by ·put stock in · appreciate ·respect ·prize ·cherish · treasure ·cherished ·treasured ·dear · prized ·esteemed ·respected ·highly regarded ·appreciated ·important

I look at the definition of value and I sit amazed thinking where do I start? We live in a time where value is only placed on me.

"Traitors, heady, high-minded, lovers of pleasures more than lovers of God;"

King James Version (KJV)

2 Timothy 3:4 Context

1This know also, that in the last days
perilous times shall come. 2For men shall
be lovers of their own selves, covetous,
boasters, proud, blasphemers,
disobedient to parents, unthankful,
unholy, 3Without natural affection,
trucebreakers, false accusers, incontinent,
fierce, despisers of those that are good,
4Traitors, heady, high-minded, lovers of
pleasures more than lovers of God;
5Having a form of godliness, but denying
the power thereof: from such turn away.
6For of this sort are they which creep into
houses, and lead captive silly women
laden with sins, led away with divers
lusts, 7Ever learning, and never able to
come to the knowledge of the truth.

I am thinking of a time in the mid 1980's after I had recommitted my life to Jesus. I received the baptism of the Holy Spirit with the evidence of speaking in tongues. The Spirit of God began using me in His manifestations before I had an understanding of what they were. I was excited because I was hearing the voice of my Father God working through me to encourage, lift up, and exhort His children in righteousness. I went to the pastor's place of business which he worked during the week to support himself so he could preach Sunday. I was excited as I shared how God was using me. I wasn't prepared for the response I got. "Why would God use you when there is someone like me around?" responded the pastor. My excitement turned into sadness and embarrassment as I walked out of the Pastor's business with my head hung down in shame.

I walked over to a friend's place and told them the story. They were shocked that the pastor responded that way. They encouraged me by saying, "that's why Gods is using you, because there is someone like him around." It wasn't long before I left that church. I couldn't understand why he felt so threatened. He, being an older Christian and being in ministry should be glad to see a young Christian man developing a close relationship with his creator to the point of being used. But this was not the case. I soon realized that many but not all Pastors thought of themselves as God's man of the hour and greater than us simple laymen. The 1980's was a unique time. I travelled to many provinces and visited many churches. It seemed like the churches were in competition with each other.

I would go to one church and hear messages condemning the church across the river. So naturally I would go check out the church across the river. I would hear a message on how you would get devils of deception if you attended the other church. Church leaders seemed to think that some scriptures don't apply to them.

1 Peter 3:8 finally, *be ye* all of one mind,
having compassion one of another, love
as brethren, *be* pitiful, *and be* courteous:
9Not rendering evil for evil, or railing for
railing: but contrariwise blessing;
knowing that ye are thereunto called,
that ye should inherit a blessing.

10For him that will love life, and see
good days, let him refrain his tongue
from evil, and his lips that they speak no
guile:

Philippians 2:3King James Version (KJV)

3 Let nothing be done through strife or vainglory; but in lowliness of mind let each esteems other better than themselves.

Philippians 2:3New International Version (NIV)

3 Do nothing out of selfish ambition or vain conceit. Rather, in humility value others above yourselves,

To get our value from church leadership could be very detriment or harmful. It seems that many organizations are into empire building rather than kingdom building. What's the difference you may ask? Empire building is building the corporate structure at the expense of people. People take a back seat to the corporation. Kingdom building is people building; building up an individual so they can fulfill their destiny in Christ is the will of God in action.

Another area we look for value is our spouses. I know of a situation where the husband had great value when he was able to work and pay for everything. One day things changed; he became disabled and could not pay for everything. He could still pay for most of the household expenses but needed some input from his wife. The wife became upset because she had to help. She decided to stop talking to her husband and ignored him completely like he never existed. That seemed a bit harsh because the bible says:

Ephesians 5:22-33New International Version (NIV)

22 Wives, submit yourselves to your own
husbands as you do to the Lord. 23 For the
husband is the head of the wife as Christ
is the head of the church, his body, of
which he is the Saviour. 24 Now as the
church submits to Christ, so also wives

should submit to their husbands in everything.

1 Peter 3 Worldwide English (New Testament) (WE)

3 Wives, respect and obey your husbands in the same way. Then the husbands who do not obey the word of God will want to know God. They will want to know God because their wives live good lives, even though they say nothing about God.
2 They will see that you live holy lives and respect your husbands.
3 You should not be fine on the outside only. Some women make their hair nice. They wear gold things. They have fine clothes.
4 But you must be fine in your heart. Have a heart that is gentle and quiet. That will not wear out. And God thinks it is worth very much.

New King James Version James 1:19-20

19So then, my beloved brethren, let every man be swift to hear, slow to speak, slow to wrath; 20for the wrath of man does not produce the righteousness of God.

I would have to ask the wife what value you placed on the husband which caused you to marry him. Did you value him for who he was or for what he could do for you? To the husband I would ask; now that your wife devalued you, how are you going to let it affect you? Just sitting thinking about this situation wondering how would I counsel the couple if they approached me. Well I guess every situation has roots so I would explore that avenue. I soon found she had a prophecy over her that she would marry a pastor and be a pastor's wife. Her response to that prophecy was I can do that job and he can be a pastor's husband.

That reminded me of a situation of a bible college student who was friends with another student. They had a good friendship going that may have developed into something more. The female was in the middle of a divorce and she was attending Bible College to find her future husband. She was determined that her next husband was going to be a pastor. When she asked her friend he wasn't sure about pastor because he was exploring the prophetic side of his nature. After Bible College they continued to communicate through email. He decided that pastor was not for him and he emailed her his decision. Her response was to cancel her email and not communicate with him again. Both women seemed to want a man for what they could do for them and how they would look in other women's eyes. Men, you do well and make me look good and I will be with you. If there ever is a time when you are unable then I am out of here maybe not physically but emotionally. As I was meditating these situations I was reminded of another church I attended for a short time.

This church was unique in its makeup. All the leadership team including the pastor was women. When I researched the organization I found the leader was a man always running for political office. He had churches worldwide in which the women were in leadership. No one got paid but all money from donations in these churches went to him making him wealthy. The men in this organization were subservient to the women. If there was a convention the men would drive the women leaders and then have to sleep on the floor or couch in the hotel room. Again I left this organization after about a year.

What is this world coming to? Some religions take the value of women and demean them and some segments of the Christian religion are making men their servants. I can't do anything about other religions but I can speak into Christianity. As Christians the bible has to be our main source.

Romans 15:4King James Version (KJV)

4 for whatsoever things were written aforetime were written for our learning, that we through patience and comfort of the scriptures might have hope.

Not only do we have to read the scriptures but we have applied them to our lives.

James 1:21-25King James Version (KJV)

21 Wherefore lay apart all filthiness and superfluity of naughtiness, and receive with meekness the engrafted word, which is able to save your souls.

22 But be ye doers of the word, and not
hearers only, deceiving your own selves.

23 For if any be a hearer of the word, and
not a doer, he is like unto a man
beholding his natural face in a glass:

24 For he beholdeth himself, and goeth his
way, and straightway forgetteth what
manner of man he was.

25 But whoso looketh into the perfect law
of liberty, and continueth therein, he
being not a forgetful hearer, but a doer of
the work, this man shall be blessed in his
deed.

James 1:21-25New King James Version (NKJV)

Doers—Not Hearers Only

21 Therefore lay aside all filthiness and
overflow of wickedness, and receive with
meekness the implanted word, which is
able to save your souls.

22 But be doers of the word and not
hearers only, deceiving yourselves. 23 For
if anyone is a hearer of the word and not
a doer, he is like a man observing his
natural face in a mirror; 24 for he observes
himself, goes away, and immediately
forgets what kind of man he was. 25 But
he who looks into the perfect law of
liberty and continues *in it,* and is not a
forgetful hearer but a doer of the work,
this one will be blessed in what he does.

I think the reason we have problems with value is because we look to men and men's religious organizations to find it. What we fail to realize is that most, not all, have me at the center of the equation. What makes me look good? What makes my organization look good? And having me in the center I will naturally show partiality.

James 2New King James Version (NKJV)

Beware of Personal Favouritism

2 My brethren, do not hold the faith of
our Lord Jesus Christ, *the Lord* of glory,
with partiality. [2] For if there should come
into your assembly a man with gold
rings, in fine apparel, and there should
also come in a poor man in filthy clothes,
[3] and you pay attention to the one
wearing the fine clothes and say to him,
"You sit here in a good place," and say to
the poor man, "You stand there," or, "Sit
here at my footstool," [4] have you not
shown partiality among yourselves, and
become judges with evil thoughts?

[5] Listen, my beloved brethren: Has God
not chosen the poor of this world *to be*
rich in faith and heirs of the kingdom
which He promised to those who love
Him? [6] But you have dishonoured the
poor man. Do not the rich oppress you
and drag you into the courts? [7] Do they

not blaspheme that noble name by which
you are called?

8 If you really fulfil *the* royal law
according to the Scripture, "You shall
love your neighbour as yourself," you do
well; 9 but if you show partiality, you
commit sin, and are convicted by the law
as transgressors. 10 For whoever shall
keep the whole law, and yet stumble in
one *point,* he is guilty of all. 11 For He who
said, "Do not commit adultery," also
said, "Do not murder." Now if you do
not commit adultery, but you do murder,
you have become a transgressor of the
law. 12 So speak and so do as those who
will be judged by the law of liberty. 13 For
judgment is without mercy to the one
who has shown no mercy. Mercy
triumphs over judgment.

Mercy triumphs over judgment reminds me of a dream I had while working for domino's pizza. The dream started with me sitting in my car parked on Main Street when a police officer opened my car door and sat in the passenger seat. We had a friendly conversation about the weather and family. He opened the door to get out and he turned to me and handed me a ticket. I asked what this is for. He responded, "You delivered a pizza to the police station and you were rude and inconsiderate." I immediately responded you made a mistake it must have been another driver. I am taking this to court. The next scene in the dream was a court house where God the Father was the judge. A female police officer was sitting in the accuser box and the judge asked her to point out the culprit and she pointed to me. When she pointed to me; my lawyer Jesus stood up and said, "I know William and he walks in the fruit of the Spirit. " As soon as he said that; the judge hit his gavel on the desk and said case dismissed. He turned to the police and said, "Be careful because the same surveillance system that is monitoring William is monitoring you. The dream ended.

I believe this is the interpretation of the dream. The first police officer was a male in my car was the accuser. The female officer in the court room represented the law which is in submission to the fruit of the spirit. If you don't walk in the spirit then your judgment is the law. Jesus was my lawyer and we see this in the Bible. 1 John 2:1 King James Bible
My little children, these things write I unto you, that ye sin not. And if any man sin, we have an advocate with the Father, Jesus Christ the righteous:
Advocate is another word for lawyer. We are the righteousness of God in Christ Jesus because of the blood of Jesus.

I believe the whole value issue can be solved by walking in the fruit of the spirit.

Galatians 5:22-23King James Version (KJV)

[22] But the fruit of the Spirit is love, joy, peace, longsuffering, gentleness, goodness, faith,

[23] Meekness, temperance: against such there is no law.

Galatians 5:22-23New International Version (NIV)

[22] But the fruit of the Spirit is love, joy,
peace, forbearance, kindness, goodness,
faithfulness, [23] gentleness and self-
control. Against such things there is no
law.

FRUIT OF THE SPIRIT

I believe you can put the nine fruit of the Spirit in three categories the same way you do the manifestations of the Spirit. The first three love, joy, and peace you develop in your life for yourself. Let me explain. If you don't have these three dominating your life you cannot be a witness to others.

1. **LOVE**

Wikipedia definitions

Need/gift love

Taking his start from St. John's words "*God is Love*", Lewis initially thought to contrast "Need-love" (such as the love of a child for its mother) and "Gift-love" (epitomized by God's love for humanity), to the disparagement of the former. However he swiftly happened on the insight that the natures of even these basic categorizations of love are more complicated than they at first seemed: a child's need for parental comfort is a necessity, not a selfish indulgence, while conversely parental Gift-love in excessive form can be a perversion of its own.

Pleasures

Lewis continued his examination by exploring the nature of pleasure, distinguishing Need-pleasures (such as water for the thirsty) from Pleasures of Appreciation, such as the love of nature. From the latter, he developed what he called "a third element in love...Appreciative love", to go along with Need-love and Gift-love.

Throughout the rest of the book, Lewis would go on to counterpart that three-fold, qualitative distinction against the four broad types of loves indicated in his title.

In his remaining four chapters, Lewis treats of love under four categories ("the highest does not stand without the lowest"), based in part on the four Greek words for *love*: affection, friendship, Eros, and charity. Lewis states that just as Lucifer (a former archangel) perverted himself by pride and fell into depravity, so too can love—commonly held to be the arch-emotion—become corrupt by presuming itself to be what it is not.

Storage—empathy bond

Storage (storgē, Greek: στοργή) is liking someone through the fondness of familiarity, family members or people who relate in familiar ways that have otherwise found themselves bonded by chance. An example is the natural love and affection of a parent for their child. It is described as the most natural, emotive, and widely diffused of loves: natural in that it is present without coercion;

emotive because it is the result of fondness due to familiarity; and most widely diffused because it pays the least attention to those characteristics deemed "valuable" or worthy of love and, as a result, is able to transcend most discriminating factors. Lewis describes it as a dependency-based love which risks extinction if the needs cease to be met.

Affection, for Lewis, included both Need-love and Gift-love. He considered it responsible for 9/10th of all solid and lasting human happiness.

Ironically, however, affection's strength is also what makes it vulnerable. Affection has the appearance of being "built-in" or "readymade", says Lewis, and as a result people come to expect it irrespective of their behavior and its natural consequences. Both in its Need and its Gift form, affection then is liable to "go bad", and to be corrupted by such forces as jealousy, ambivalence and smothering.

Philia – friend bond

Philia (philía, Greek: φιλία) is the love between friends as close as siblings in strength and duration. The friendship is the strong bond existing between people who share common values, interests or activities. Lewis immediately differentiates friendship love from the other loves. He describes friendship as "the least biological, organic, instinctive, gregarious and necessary...the least *natural* of loves". Our species does not need friendship in order to reproduce, but to the classical and medieval worlds it is a higher-level love because it is freely chosen.

Lewis explains that true friendships, like the friendship between David and Jonathan in the Bible, are almost a lost art. He expresses a strong distaste for the way modern society ignores friendship. He notes that he cannot remember any poem that celebrated true friendship like that between David and Jonathan, Orestes and Pylades, Roland and Oliver, Amis and Amiles. Lewis goes on to say, "to the Ancients, Friendship seemed the happiest and most fully human of all loves; the crown of life and the school of virtue. The modern world, in comparison, ignores it".

Growing out of companionship, friendship for Lewis was a deeply appreciative love, though one which he felt few people in modern society could value at its worth, because so few actually experienced true friendship.

Nevertheless, Lewis was not blind to the dangers of friendships, such as its potential for cliques, anti-authoritarianism and pride.

Eros – erotic bond

Eros (erōs, Greek: ἔρως) for Lewis was love in the sense of "being in love" or "loving" someone, as opposed to the raw sexuality of what he called Venus: the illustration Lewis used was the distinction between "wanting a woman" and wanting one particular woman – something that matched his (classical) view of man as a rational animal, a composite both of reasoning angel and instinctual alley-cat.

Eros turns the need-pleasure of Venus into the most appreciative of all pleasures; but nevertheless Lewis warned against the modern tendency for Eros to become a god to people who fully submit themselves to it, a justification for selfishness, even a phallic religion.

After exploring sexual activity and its spiritual significance in both a pagan and a Christian sense, he notes how Eros (or being in love) is in itself an indifferent, neutral force: how "Eros in his entire splendor...may urge to evil as well as good". While accepting that Eros can be an extremely profound experience, he does not overlook the dark way in which it could lead even to the point of suicide pacts or murder, as well as to furious refusals to part, "mercilessly chaining together two mutual tormentors, each raw all over with the poison of hate-in-love".

Agape – unconditional "God" love

Charity (agápē, Greek: ἀγάπη) is the love that exists regardless of changing circumstances. Lewis recognizes this one as the greatest of the four loves, and sees it as a specifically Christian virtue to achieve. The chapter on the subject focuses on the need to subordinate the other three natural loves—as Lewis puts it, "The natural loves are not self-sufficient"—to the love of God, who is full of charitable love, to prevent what he termed their "demonic" self-aggrandizement. Lewis did not actually use the word "*agape*", although later commentators did.

Of all the types of love listed I believe Agape is the love mentioned in Galatians 5:22. To develop this love in our life we need a revelation of God's love for us….humanity. When we have a revelation of God's love for me how can I not help love those who God loves and treat them with grace and kindness.

Bible verses about God's love for us

Many of us have a hard time understanding the love of God. I personally have struggled with understanding His great love for me. I used to live like His love was dependent on my performance on my walk of faith, which is idolatry. My mindset was, "I have to do something to make God love me more."

When I sin that sin that I struggle with or when I don't pray or read Scripture I have to make up for it by doing something, which is a lie from Satan.

If you are a Christian I want you to understand that you are loved. His love for you is not based upon your performance.

It's based upon the perfect merit of Jesus Christ. You don't have to move at all you are loved. You don't have to be big. You don't have to be the next Billy Graham or Billye Brim or Kenneth Hagin. You just have to be yourself. God loves you and don't you ever forget that.

Don't you dare think for a second that you can love anyone more than God loves you.

Quotes

- "God loves you more in a moment than anyone could in a lifetime."
- "One who has been touched by grace will no longer look on those who stray as 'those evil people' or 'those poor people who need our help.' Nor must we search for signs of 'love worthiness.' Grace teaches us that God loves because of who God is, not because of who we are." Philip Yancey

- "Though our feelings come and go, God's love for us does not." C.S. Lewis
- "Christ is the humility of God embodied in human nature; the Eternal Love humbling itself, clothing itself in the garb of meekness and gentleness, to win and serve and save us." Andrew Murray

Take a look at this verse. Marriage shows the relationship between Christ and the church. This verse shows how much God loves you. One look upward and you have the Lord hooked. He wants to be with you and when you enter into His presence His heart beats faster.

1. Song of Solomon 4:9 "You have made my heart beat faster, my sister, my bride; you have made my heart beat faster with

a single glance of your eyes, with a single strand of your necklace."

Where does love come from? How are you able to love your mother, father, child, friends, etc? God's love is so powerful that we are able to love others. Think about how parents see their newborn child and smile. Think about parents playing with their children and having a good time. Have you ever thought about where does that stuff come from? These things are here to be representations to show how much God loves and is joyful over His children.

2. 1 John 4:19 "We love because He first loved us."

3. 1 John 4:16 "And so we know and rely on the love God has for us. God is love. Whoever lives in love lives in God, and God in them?"

4. 1 John 4:7 "Dear friends, let us love one another, for love comes from God. Everyone who loves has been born of God and knows God."

True love takes action. God poured out His awesome love for us on the cross. He crushed His Son so that you may live. When you allow your joy and peace to come from the perfect merit of Christ you will understand God's love better. It is not dependent on what you do, what you are going to do, or what you have done. God's love is greatly shown by what He has already done for you.

5. 1 John 4:10 "This is love: not that we loved God, but that he loved us and sent his Son as an atoning sacrifice for our sins."

6. Romans 5:8-9 "But God demonstrates his own love for us in this: While we were still sinners, Christ died for us. Since we have now been justified by

his blood, how much more shall we be saved from God's wrath through him!"

7. John 3:16 "For God so loved the world, that he gave his only begotten Son, that whosoever believeth in him should not perish, but have everlasting life."

True believers have the love of God in them.

8. John 5:40-43 "yet you refuse to come to me to have life. 'I do not accept glory from human beings, but I know you. I know that you do not have the love of God in your hearts. I have come in my Father's name, and you do not accept me; but if someone else comes in his own name, you will accept him."

9. Romans 5:5 "And hope does not put us to shame, because God's love has been poured out into our hearts through the Holy Spirit, who has been given to us."

Pray for a greater understanding of the love of God. Sometimes it is so hard to grasp His love for us especially when we look into the mirror and see all of our failures. Without knowing how much God loves you, you are going to feel so miserable.

I was praying one night and I was thinking to myself that God wants me to do more, no! The whole time that I was praying I didn't understand that all God wanted for me was to just understand His great love for me. I don't have to move a muscle I am loved.

10. 2 Thessalonians 3:5 "May the Lord lead your hearts into a full understanding and expression of the love of God and the patient endurance that comes from Christ."

God is not mad at you. Whenever you think that you have done something to separate yourself from God's love or it's too late to get right with God or you need to be more to be loved of God remember that nothing can separate God's love for you. Always remember that God's love never ends.

11. Psalm 136:2-3 "Give thanks to the God of gods, for his steadfast love endures forever. Give thanks to the Lord of lords: His love endures forever. To him who alone do great wonders, His love endures forever."

12. 1 Corinthians 13:8 "Love will never end. But all those gifts will come to an end—even the gift of prophecy, the gift of speaking in different kinds of languages, and the gift of knowledge."

13. Psalm 36:7 "How precious is your unfailing love, O God! **All humanity**

finds shelter in the shadow of your wings."

14. Psalm 109:26 "Help me, LORD my God; save me according to your unfailing love."

15. Romans 8:38-39 "And I am convinced that nothing can ever separate us from God's love. Neither death nor life, neither angels nor demons, neither our fears for today nor our worries about tomorrow–not even the powers of hell can separate us from God's love. No power in the sky above or in the earth below–indeed, nothing in all creation will ever be able to separate us from the love of God that is revealed in Christ Jesus our Lord."

The love of God compels us to do His will. It is the love of God that drives me to keep fighting and obeying Him. It is the love of God that allows me to discipline myself and it gives me a desire to keep pushing when struggling with sin. The love of God transforms us.

16. 2 Corinthians 5:14-15 "For Christ's love compels us, because we are convinced that one died for all, and therefore all died. And he died for all, that those who live should no longer live for themselves but for him who died for them and was raised again."

17. Galatians 2:20 "I have been crucified with Christ and I no longer live, but Christ lives in me. The life I now live in the body, I live by faith in the Son of God, who loved me and gave himself for me."

18. Ephesians 2:2-5 "in which you formerly lived according to this world's present path, according to the ruler of the kingdom of the air, the ruler of the spirit that is now energizing the sons of disobedience, among whom all of us also formerly lived out our lives in the cravings of our flesh, indulging the

desires of the flesh and the mind, and were by nature children of wrath even as the rest. But God, being rich in mercy, because of his great love with which he loved us, even though we were dead in transgressions, made us alive together with Christ—by grace you are saved!"

It was the love of God that drove Jesus when everyone was yelling, "crucify Him." It was the love of God that drove Jesus to keep going in humiliation and pain. With every step and with every drop of blood the love of God drove Jesus to do the will of His Father.

19. John 19:1-3 "Then Pilate took Jesus and had him flogged severely. The soldiers braided a crown of thorns and put it on his head, and they clothed him in a purple robe. They came up to him again and again and said, "Hail, king of

the Jews!" And they struck him repeatedly in the face."

Discipline shows the great love that God has for His children. Like a loving parent He makes sure that you remain on the right path. God says, "I love you and I refuse to let you live like wicked unbelievers."

20. Hebrews 12:6 "For **the Lord disciplines the one he loves**, and chastises every son whom he receives."

21. Proverbs 3:12 "because the LORD disciplines those he loves, as a father the son he delights in."

God's love causes us to remain calm, stand strong, and never give up.

22. 1 Corinthians 13:7 "Love never gives up on people. It never stops trusting, never loses hope, and never quits."

23. Jude 1:21 "keep yourselves in the love of God, waiting for the mercy of our Lord Jesus Christ that leads to eternal life."

24. Zephaniah 3:17 "The LORD your God is in your midst, A victorious warrior. He will exult over you with joy, He will be quiet in His love, He will rejoice over you with shouts of joy."

25. 1 Peter 5:6-7 " And God will exalt you in due time, if you humble yourselves under his mighty hand by casting all your cares on him because he cares for you."

Get the picture? If God loves me then I should love me and love what God Loves and hate what God hates. When you get a revelation of God's love for you and mankind it is easier to love others.

The next fruit listed is joy and definitely needed in people's lives. If you are sad and depressed how can you share Jesus with them? Come receive Jesus as your savior and he will make you as depressed as I am. Nobody will buy that bag of goodies. Let's see what the bible says about joy.

Bible Verses about Joy

Here is what we learn from our Bible verses about joy.

1. Joy is not an emotion that can be forced, fabricated, or faked.

There are times when joy eludes us. This is normal and we need to understand that there are times when we will not feel joyful. Yet, it is important that joy cannot be forced.

There on the poplars we hung our harps, for there our captors asked us for songs, our tormentors demanded songs of joy; they said, "Sing us one of the songs of Zion!" How can we sing the songs of the Lord while in a foreign land? – Psalm 137:2-4 (NIV).

2. Joy is not dependent upon our circumstance

For in the day of trouble he will keep me safe in his dwelling; he will hide me in the shelter of his sacred tent and set me high upon a rock. Then my head will be exalted above the enemies who surround me; at his sacred tent I will sacrifice with shouts of joy; I will sing and make music to the Lord. Hear my voice when I call, Lord; be merciful to me and answer me. – Psalm 27:5-7 (NIV).

We can be in a difficult situation and yet experience joy. Jesus added to this by saying, "Blessed are you when people hate you, when they exclude you and insult you and reject your name as evil, because of the Son of Man. Rejoice in that day and leap for joy, because great is your reward in heaven. For that is how their ancestors treated the prophets." – Luke 6:22-23 (NIV)

Though joy cannot be forced, it can be experienced in difficult situations. James adds to this thought with, "Consider it pure joy, my brothers and sisters, whenever you face trials of many kinds, because you know that the testing of your faith produces perseverance." – James 1:2-3 (NIV).

3. Joy is possible when we feel secure in the Lord.

Many, Lord, are asking, "Who will bring us prosperity?" Let the light of your face shine on us. Fill my heart with joy when their grain and new wine abound. In peace I will lie down and sleep, for you alone, Lord, make me dwell in safety. – Psalm 4:6-8

While others link their happiness to prosperity, believers can find joy in the Lord. When we add our voice to David's and proclaim, "You alone, Lord," will be the lifter of my head. In you alone will I place my trust? Whether I am rich or poor have an active career, or I can't find a job, I am safe in you.

Paul wrote, "Be full of joy in the Lord always. I will say again, be full of joy. Let everyone see that you are gentle and kind. The Lord is coming soon" Philippians 4:4-5 (NCV).

4. Joy comes when we have a clear direction for our life.

We might also use the word purpose. The following verses about joy illustrate this principle:

You make known to me the path of life; you will fill me with joy in your presence, with eternal pleasures at your right hand. – Psalm 16:11 (NIV)
Jesus said, "The kingdom of heaven is like treasure hidden in a field. When a man found it, he hid it again, and then in his joy went and sold all he had and bought that field" – Matthew 13:44 (NIV).

Where is your hidden treasure? What is the path of life that God has for you? Are you seeking the fields for the treasure that God has for you?

5. Joy comes when we live in God's presence.

Through the victories you gave, his glory is great; you have bestowed on him splendor and majesty. Surely you have granted him unending blessings and made him glad with the joy of your presence. For the king trusts in the Lord; through the unfailing love of the Most High he will not be shaken. – Psalm 21:5-7 (NIV).

In a world where celebrity, success, and money are glorified, it is easy to lose focus on what brings real joy. Put simply, this verse says, victories are good, glory is great, and splendor and majesty are their results, but my joy comes when I spend time in God's presence.

Psalm 28:6-8 is another great text to illustrate this point, but let's move joy Bible verses found in the New Testament.

To him who is able to keep you from stumbling and to present you before his glorious presence without fault and with great joy – to the only God our Savior be glory, majesty, power and authority, through Jesus Christ our Lord, before all ages, now and forevermore! Amen – Jude 1:2-5 (NIV). *How can we thank God enough for you in return for all the joy we have in the presence of our God because of you?* – 1 Thessalonians 3:9 (NIV).

6. Joy comes when we spend our life praising God.

This principle may be the easiest one to embrace since church worship is filled with praise. But, let's establish a Biblical pattern of praise.

And now my head shall be lifted up above my enemies all around me; therefore I will offer sacrifices of joy in His tabernacle; I will sing, yes, I will sing praises to the Lord. – Psalm 27:6 (NKJV)

My lips will shout for joy when I sing praise to you – I whom you have delivered. – Psalm 71:23

Singing and shouting are all a part of joyful worship. These three Bible verses about joy only scratch the surface of examples of praise. Here is another example of praise found in Luke, "As he went along, people spread their cloaks on the road. When he came near the place where the road goes down the Mount of Olives, the whole crowd of disciples began joyfully to praise God in loud voices for all the miracles they had seen: "Blessed is the king who comes in the name of the Lord!" "Peace in heaven and glory in the highest!" – Luke 19:36-39 (NIV).

Joy is an important part of the Christian life. Many believers do not have a revelation of joy and how powerful it is in their lives. Let's look at the definition of joy.

Joy

1. A deep feeling or condition of happiness or contentment
2. Something causing such a feeling; a source of happiness
3. An outward show of pleasure or delight; rejoicing
4. Success; satisfaction:

Not only do we express joy for whom God is and what Jesus did for us at the cross. We express joy on behalf of other people. When people excel in their relationship with God and express themselves don't be envious but rejoice with them. When joy is expressed in your life you attract people. One of the definitions is contentment. This reminds me of meetings that I have been in where everybody breaks out in uncontrollable laughter. Everyone except me, I sit there totally at peace with a sense of contentment. People look at me funny and ask why am I not experiencing the joy of the Lord? I was a bit confused until I heard a preacher say, "peace is joy at rest and joy is peace expressed." I have laughed two or three times in my life but mostly when God is moving strong I just sit there totally at peace and content.

Nehemiah 8:10, King James Bible
Then he said unto them, Go your way, eat the fat, and drink the sweet, and send portions unto them for whom nothing is prepared: for *this* day *is* holy unto our Lord: neither be ye sorry; for the joy of the LORD is your strength.
Joy is such a wonderful fruit that should be in the orchard of your life so others, including yourself can partake of. Let's look at peace. Peace is the third fruit to develop in your life for yourself, here's why. If you are worried anxious and freaked out all the time you cannot be a witness of Jesus. Nobody wants what you got because they have enough problems of their own. People are looking for answers. If you are walking in peace then people will notice and be drawn to you.

The meaning of peace according to the dictionary is from a natural carnal perspective.

Peace [pēs]
NOUN
Freedom from disturbance; quiet and tranquility:
"You can while away an hour or two in peace and seclusion"
Synonyms: **tranquility** · **calm** · **restfulness** · peace and quiet · **Peacefulness** · **quiet** · **quietness** · **privacy** · **solitude**
Antonyms: **noise**
Mental calm; serenity:
"The peace of mind this insurance gives you"
synonyms: **serenity** · **peacefulness** · **tranquility** · **equanimity** · [more]**calm** · **calmness** · **composure** · **ease** · **contentment** · **contentedness**
Antonyms: **agitation** · **distress**

Freedom from or the cessation of war or violence:

"The Straits were to be open to warships in time of peace"

Synonyms: **law and order** · **lawfulness** · **order** · **peacefulness** · **Peaceableness** · **harmony** · **nonviolence** · **concord**

Antonyms: **conflict**

A period of this:

"The peace didn't last"

A treaty agreeing to the cessation of war between warring states:

"Support for a negotiated peace"

Synonyms: **treaty** · **truce** · **ceasefire** · **armistice** ·

Cessation/suspension of hostilities

Antonyms: **war**

Freedom from civil disorder:

"Police action to restore peace"

Synonyms: **law and order** · **lawfulness** · **order** · **peacefulness** ·

Peaceableness · harmony · nonviolence · concord
Antonyms: **conflict**
Freedom from dispute or dissension between individuals or groups:
"The 8.8 percent offer that promises peace with the board"
(The peace)
A ceremonial handshake or kiss exchanged during a service in some churches (now usually only in the Eucharist), symbolizing Christian love and unity. See also **kiss of peace** at **kiss**.
EXCLAMATION
Used as a greeting.
Used as an order to remain silent.

In a large majority of cases, the word peace in the Bible is the Hebrew word shalom... While the literal translation is peace - the meaning of shalom is far more than simply the absence of war. In the Hebrew understanding, shalom is being in harmony with God and all of God's creation.

2 Thessalonians 3:16 - Now the Lord of peace himself give you peace always by all means. The Lord [be] with you all.

John 16:33 - These things I have spoken unto you, that in me ye might have peace. In the world ye shall have tribulation: but be of good cheer; I have overcome the world.

Philippians 4:6 - Be careful for nothing; but in everything by prayer and supplication with thanksgiving let your requests be made known unto God.

Isaiah 26:3 - Thou wilt keep [him] in perfect peace, [whose] mind [is] stayed [on thee]: because he trusteth in thee.

1 Peter 5:7 - Casting all your care upon him; for he careth for you.

Matthew 5:9 - Blessed [are] the

peacemakers: for they shall be called the children of God.

Romans 12:18 - If it be possible, as much as lieth in you, live peaceably with all men.

Matthew 10:34-36 - Think not that I am come to send peace on earth: I came not to send peace, but a sword.

1 Peter 3:11 - Let him eschew evil, and do good; let him seek peace, and ensue it.

Romans 15:13 - Now the God of hope fill you with all joy and peace in believing, that ye may abound in hope, through the power of the Holy Ghost.

Hebrews 12:14 - Follow peace with all [men], and holiness, without which no man shall see the Lord:

1 Peter 5:6-7 - Humble yourselves

therefore under the mighty hand of God, that he may exalt you in due time:

Psalms 4:8 - I will both lay me down in peace, and sleep: for thou, LORD, only makest me dwell in safety.

Proverbs 12:20 - Deceit [is] in the heart of them that imagine evil: but to the counsellors of peace [is] joy.

Isaiah 12:2 - Behold, God [is] my salvation; I will trust, and not be afraid: for the LORD JEHOVAH [is] my strength and [my] song; he also is become my salvation.

1 Corinthians 14:33 - For God is not [the author] of confusion, but of peace, as in all churches of the saints.

Love peace and joy are like triplets that work on your behalf. All those scriptures on love joy and peace to simply say this.

Ecclesiastes 4:12 New American Standard Bible
and if one can overpower him who is alone, two can resist him. A cord of three strands is not quickly torn apart.

King James Bible
and if one prevail against him, two shall withstand him; and a threefold cord is not quickly broken.
Remember earlier I said you develop the first three fruit of the Spirit for yourself.
Love - a revelation of God's love for you and mankind sets you free to be Imitators of God

1. Ephesians 5:1-2New American Standard Bible Therefore be imitators of God, as beloved children; [2] and walk in love, just as Christ also loved [a]you and gave Himself up for us, an offering and a sacrifice to God [b]as a fragrant aroma.
2. Joy gives you strength to walk in God's love towards yourself and others

Romans 5:5 King James Bible
and hope maketh not ashamed; because the love of God is shed abroad in our hearts by the Holy Ghost which is given unto us.
Peace gives you the confidence that no matter what situations come your way it is taken care of by a loving Father.

Isaiah 26:3 - Thou wilt keep [him] in perfect peace, [whose] mind [is] stayed [on thee]: because he trusteth in thee.

If you wrap yourself in this threefold cord you will be ready to develop the next three fruit of the spirit in your life.

The next three fruit of the Spirit you develop in your life for others.

Galatians 5:22-23New International Version (NIV)

[22] But the fruit of the Spirit is love, joy, peace, forbearance, kindness, goodness, faithfulness, [23] gentleness and self-control. Against such things there is no law.

The word forbearance is also translated longsuffering in the King James Bible.

Definition of LONG-SUFFERING

: Patiently enduring lasting offense or hardship
Forbearance

[fawr-bair-uh ns]

noun
1. the act of forbearing; a refraining from something.
2. **forbearing** conduct or quality; patient endurance; self-control.
3. an abstaining from the enforcement of a right.
4. a creditor's giving of indulgence after the day originally fixed for payment.
Origin of forbearance Expand
1570-1580
First recorded in 1570-80; forbear[1]+ **-ance**
Related forms Expand
no forbearance, noun
Synonyms Expand
See more synonyms on Thesaurus.com

1. abstinence. 2. tolerance, toleration, sufferance; indulgence.
Dictionary.com Unabridged
Based on the Random House Dictionary,

Examples from the Web for forbearance
Expand
Contemporary Examples

- Parenting a preschooler is hard (believe me, I know), and it takes a lot of time, energy, and *forbearance* to do it right.
- But selfies, like people, deserve our forgiveness, our *forbearance*, and our support.

After reading the definitions can you see where I am going when I say you develop this fruit in your life for other people? You tolerate other people's issues and if their ideas differ from yours you will not enforce your right to be correct.

2 Timothy 2:24 ASV And the Lord's servant must not strive, but be gentle towards all, apt to teach, forbearing,

AMP

The servant of the Lord must not participate in quarrels, but must be kind to everyone [even-tempered, preserving peace, and he must be], skilled in teaching, patient *and* tolerant when wronged.

kindness

[ˈkīn(d)nəs]

NOUN

the quality of being friendly, generous, and considerate.

synonyms: kindliness · kindheartedness · **warm-heartedness** · affection · warmth · gentleness · concern · care · consideration · helpfulness · thoughtfulness ·

- a kind act:

"it is a kindness I shall never forget"

Synonyms: kindliness · kindheartedness · **warm-heartedness** · affection · warmth · gentleness · concern · care · consideration · helpfulness · thoughtfulness

Wouldn't you like to be known as?

KINDNESS

(Your name), the word that describes you perfectly is KIND!
Your life is too interesting to be defined in words but this one word suits you the most and you couldn't agree more. You have a great personality and many other beautiful qualities. Among other things you are Faithful and Patient.
Your friends and are also in awe of you and your amazing qualities.
You possess an extremely likable personality. No matter who comes across your path, you always get along with them. This makes you very popular and makes getting ahead in your career child's play to you. Your wonderful essence makes you a person of success!
You never judge anybody because you can empathize and understand where other people's behavior is coming from. This quality makes you a great friend.

The next fruit you develop in your life for other people is goodness. Dictionary definition of goodness is;

Goodness

[goo d-nis]

noun

1. the state or quality of being good.
2. moral excellence; virtue.
3. kindly feeling; kindness; generosity.
4. excellence of quality: goodness of workmanship.
5. the best part of anything; essence; strength.
6. A euphemism for God: Thank goodness

Dictionaries - Easton's Bible Dictionary - Goodness

Goodness

in man is not a mere passive quality, but the deliberate preference of right to wrong, the firm and persistent resistance of all moral evil, and the choosing and following of all moral good.

These dictionary topics are from M.G. Easton M.A., D.D., Illustrated Bible Dictionary, Third Edition, published by Thomas Nelson, 1897. Public Domain, copy freely.

Bibliography Information

Easton, Matthew George. "Entry for Goodness". "Easton's Bible Dictionary". .

Encyclopedia's - International Standard Bible Encyclopedia - Goodness

GOODNESS

good'-nes:

This word in the Old Testament is the translation of Tobh (Exodus 18:9; Psalms 16:2, the Revised Version (British and American) "good"; 23:6), etc.; of Tubh (Exodus 33:19; Psalms 31:19; Jeremiah 31:14; Hosea 3:5), etc.; of checedh

(Exodus 34:6), "abundant in goodness," the English Revised Version "plenteous in mercy," the American Standard Revised Version "abundant in loving kindness"; "The goodness of God endureth continually," the Revised Version (British and American) "mercy," the American Standard Revised Version "loving kindness" (Psalms 52:1), etc.

In the New Testament it is the translation of chrestotes ("usefulness," benignity); "the riches of his goodness" (Romans 2:4; 11:22, thrice); of chrestos ("useful," "benign," "kind," in Luke 6:35); "The goodness of God leadeth thee to repentance" (Romans 2:4); of agathosune (found only in the New Testament and Septuagint and writings based thereon), "full of goodness." (Romans 15:14); "gentleness, goodness, faith" (Galatians 5:22); "in all goodness and righteousness and truth" (Ephesians 5:9); "all the good pleasure of his goodness," the Revised

Version (British and American) "every desire of goodness." (2 Thessalonians 1:11).

The thought of God as good and the prominence given to "good" and "goodness" are distinctive features of the Bible. In the passage quoted above from Galatians 5:22, "goodness" is one of the fruits of the indwelling Spirit of God, and in that from Ephesians 5:9 it is described as being, along with righteousness and truth, "the fruit of the light" which Christians had been "made" in Christ. Here, as elsewhere, we are reminded that the Christian life in its truth is likeness to God, the source and perfection of all good. 2 Thessalonians 1:11 regards God Himself as expressing His goodness in and through us.

Can you see how these fruit are developed in your life for others?

(Your name), the word that describes you perfectly is LONG-SUFFERING, KIND, and GOODNESS!
Your life is too interesting to be defined in words but these words suits you the most and you couldn't agree more. You have a great personality and many other beautiful qualities. Among other things you are Faithful and Patient.
Your friends and are also in awe of you and your amazing qualities.
You possess an extremely likable personality. No matter who comes across your path, you always get along with them. Your wonderful essence makes you a person of success! You never judge anybody because you can empathize and understand where other people's behavior is coming from. You attempt to manifest God's goodness, as much as the revelation you have, to everyone that comes into your sphere of influence.
These qualities make you a great friend.

Now that you have developed the first three fruit for yourself and the second three for others, you are ready to develop the last three fruit for God. FOR GOD? WHAT ARE YOU TALKING ABOUT?

Galatians 5:22-23New International Version (NIV)

22 But the fruit of the Spirit is love, joy,
peace, forbearance, kindness, goodness,
faithfulness, 23 gentleness and self-
control. Against such things there is no
law.

Dictionary definition of FAITHFUL
1 *obsolete*: full of faith
2: steadfast in affection or allegiance: LOYAL
A *faithful* friend
3: firm in adherence to promises or in observance of duty: CONSCIENTIOUS
A *faithful* employee
4: given with strong assurance: BINDING

A *faithful* promise
5: true to the facts, to a standard, or to an original
A *faithful* copy
When I looked at this definition, I was particularly struck with the illustration used for the last definition, "true to the facts, to a standard, or to an original A *faithful* copy
For the Christian, faithfulness occurs when we allow the Lord Jesus to reproduce Himself in us or when we put on the Lord Jesus Christ and become transformed by His life.

Definition of GENTLENESS

: The quality or state of being gentle; *especially*: mildness of manners or disposition
Definition of GENTLE
Gentler play \ˈjent-lər, -tᵊl-ər\;
gentlest play \ˈjent-ləst, -tᵊl-əst\
1 a: belonging to a family of high social station

B *archaic*: CHIVALROUS
C: HONORABLE, DISTINGUISHED; *specifically*: of or relating to a gentleman
D: KIND, AMIABLE —used especially in address as a complimentary epithet
Gentle reader
E: suited to a person of high social station
The *gentle* art of sophisticated conversation
2 a: TRACTABLE, DOCILE
A *gentle* horse
B: free from harshness, sternness, or violence
Used *gentle* persuasion
3: SOFT, DELICATE
The *gentle* touch of her hand
4: MODERATE
His doctor recommended *gentle* exercise.

Gentleness

Dictionaries - Baker's Evangelical Dictionary of Biblical Theology - Gentleness

Gentleness [N]

Sensitivity of disposition and kindness of behavior founded on strength and prompted by love.

The Old Testament. Gentleness is suggested by the waters of a stream (Isa 8:6) or by wine flowing over lips and teeth (So 7:9).

It stands in contrast to baseness (Deuteronomy 28:54 Deuteronomy 28:56), harshness (2 Sam 18:5), and wildness (Job 41:3). Gentle words wield great power (Prov 15:1 ; 25:15).

Job's counsels were well received, because he spoke them gently (Job 29:22).

Gentleness evidences itself in a willingness to yield, reminiscent of a lamb being led to slaughter (Jer 11:19 ; cf. Isa 53:7). The supreme exemplar of gentleness is Israel's God. He cares tenderly for the flock under his care, and "gently leads those that have young" (Isa 40:11). He discloses himself not just in wind and earthquake and fire, but in "a gentle whisper" (1 Kings 19:11-13). His consolations are spoken gently (Job 15:11). As Yahweh's representative, the messianic king comes in humility and gentleness (Zec 9:9).

The New Testament. That king, now come in the flesh, is "gentle and humble in heart" (Matt 11:29). In accord with the prophecy, he enters Jerusalem in gentleness and lowliness (Matt 21:5). Paul appeals to believers "by the meekness and gentleness of Christ" (2 Cor 10:1). By his Spirit, Christ cultivates the same quality in his people (Gal 5:23). Following Jesus' example, Paul treats his people gently, "like a mother caring for her little children" (1 Thess 2:7). He comes to them not "with a whip [but] in love and with a gentle spirit" (1 Cor 4:21). Church leaders are admonished to be "not violent but gentle" toward persons under their care (1 Tim 3:3); it is a quality they are avidly to pursue (1 Tim 6:11). Knowing themselves to be subject to weakness, they can more readily deal gently with the ignorant and the erring. Believers ensnared by sin must be restored gently (Gal 6:1). A witness to

Christian truth is the more effective for being made "with gentleness and respect, " especially toward a hostile or an unbelieving listener (2 Tim 2:25 ; 1 Peter 3:15). The qualities to which gentleness is joined elucidate its setting and character. Wives should seek "the unfading beauty of a gentle and quiet spirit" (1 Peter 3:4). "Be completely humble and gentle; be patient, bearing with one another in love, " exhorts Paul (Eph 4:2). Let believers clothe themselves "with compassion, kindness, humility, gentleness and patience" (Col 3:12). "The fruit of the Spirit is love, joy, peace, patience, kindness, goodness, faithfulness, gentleness and self-control" (Gal 5:22-23), a cluster of qualities each of which reinforces and finds expression in the others.

J. Knox Chamblin

Gentleness evidences itself in a willingness to yield to the Holy Spirit. Many Christians resist the Holy Spirit unconsciously not realizing they are limiting their lives to a religious paradigm of weakness and defeat. By yielding to the Holy Spirit he helps us to be more Christ like.

Self-control

The ability to control ones own action, behavior, feelings, emotions, reaction, response, thoughts and will.

What does self-control mean?

Self-denial, self-discipline, self-control (noun)

The act of denying yourself; controlling your impulses

Self-control, self-possession, possession, willpower, will power, self-command, self-will (noun)

The trait of resolutely controlling your own behavior

Self-control (Noun)

The ability to control one's desires and impulses; willpower.

In the King James self-control is called temperance.

Galatians 5:22-23King James Version (KJV)

22 But the fruit of the Spirit is love, joy, peace, longsuffering, gentleness, goodness, faith,

23 Meekness, temperance: against such there is no law.

Temperance

Galatians 5:23, defines temperance as: "*the dominion which one has over oneself or something.... the dominion that one has over his thoughts, words, and actions*
As Paul said, "*...bringing into captivity every thought to the obedience of Christ*" (2 Corinthians 10:5). That is temperance

You definitely need to develop self-control in your life for God. When God begins to manifest himself in your life it can be overwhelming emotionally. You may have an impulse to do something or get over excited and find out you grieved the Holy Spirit. I've been in meetings where the Spirit of God is in manifestation and excitement was increasing then people began to cheer and clap and suddenly the atmosphere changed and no more manifestations of the Holy Spirit. I have also been in meetings where the minister would lay hands on people and deliberately push them over as if the power of God knocked them down. This minister not only got contempt for himself by the people he pushed over but showed sinners who don't know better a negative side to God.

The fruit of the Spirit you develop in your life for God. Faithfulness, gentleness and self-control"

1. Faithfulness: For the Christian, faithfulness occurs when we allow the Lord Jesus to reproduce Himself in us or when we put on the Lord Jesus Christ and become transformed by His life.
2. Gentleness: Gentleness evidences itself in a willingness to yield to the Holy Spirit
3. Self-control-Temperance: bringing into captivity every thought and action to the obedience of Christ.

In conclusion: the value issue solved

1. Remember earlier I said you develop the first three fruit of the Spirit for yourself.
   Love - Joy - Peace

If you wrap yourself in this threefold cord then you will be ready to develop the next three fruit of the Spirit. You have your value from God and have no need to look to man for value but can now be a giver of value.

2. Remember I said the next three you develop for others. Forbearance (long-suffering)-kindness- goodness. If you develop these then this could apply to your life.
   <u>(Your name),</u> the words that describes you perfectly is LONG-SUFFERING, KIND, and GOODNESS!
   Your life is too interesting to be

defined in words but these words suits you the most and you couldn't agree more. You have a great personality and many other beautiful qualities. Among other things you are Faithful and Patient. Your friends and are also in awe of you and your amazing qualities. You possess an extremely likable personality. No matter who comes across your path, you always get along with them. Your wonderful essence makes you a person of success! You never judge anybody because you can empathize and understand where other people's behaviour is coming from. You attempt to manifest God's goodness, as much as the revelation you have, to everyone that comes into your sphere of influence. These qualities make you a great friend.

3. The fruit of the Spirit you develop in your life for God. Faithfulness, gentleness and self-control"
This makes you more Christ like with the mind of Christ

A NEW LIFE
To Him (Jesus) be glory and honor forever

Father I ask for forgiveness for living a carnal religious life. I have been looking to men for value. I have been involved in a works mentality in the church to find my value. I am guilty of thinking that by taking courses offered by the church and get a certificate and applause from men, that I gain merit with you. I realize church work is important but does not give me my value. Help me to realize my value comes through Jesus Christ. Help me to realize my works come through my relationship with Jesus not to earn merits and approval from Jesus. Help me to look to the word of God and your love for my value and not the fleeting whims of mankind.

Galatians 3King James Version (KJV)

3 O foolish Galatians, who hath
bewitched you, that ye should not obey
the truth, before whose eyes Jesus Christ
hath been evidently set forth, crucified
among you?

2 This only would I learn of you, Received
ye the Spirit by the works of the law, or
by the hearing of faith?

3 Are ye so foolish? Having begun in the
Spirit, are ye now made perfect by the
flesh?

4 Have ye suffered so many things in
vain? If it be yet in vain.

5 He therefore that ministereth to you the
Spirit, and worketh miracles among you,
doeth he it by the works of the law, or by
the hearing of faith?

6 Even as Abraham believed God, and it
was accounted to him for righteousness.

7 Know ye therefore that they which are
of faith, the same are the children of
Abraham.

8 And the scripture, foreseeing that God
would justify the heathen through faith,
preached before the gospel unto
Abraham, saying in thee shall all nations
be blessed.

9 So then they which be of faith are
blessed with faithful Abraham.

10 For as many as are of the works of the
law are under the curse: for it is written,
Cursed is every one that continueth not
in all things which are written in the
book of the law to do them.

11 But that no man is justified by the law
in the sight of God, it is evident: for, the
just shall live by faith.

Romans 1 16 For I am not ashamed of
the gospel of Christ: for it is the power of
God unto salvation to everyone that
believeth; to the Jew first, and also to the
Greek.

17 For therein is the righteousness of God
revealed from faith to faith: as it is
written, the just shall live by faith.

Father I realize walking by faith is walking in the Spirit.

Question: "What does it mean to walk in the Spirit?"

Answer: Believers have the Spirit of Christ, the hope of glory within them (Colossians 1:27). Those who walk in the Spirit will show forth daily, moment-by-moment holiness. This is brought about by consciously choosing by faith to rely on the Holy Spirit to guide in thought, word, and deed (Romans 6:11-14). Failure to rely on the Holy Spirit's guidance will result in a believer not living up to the calling and standing that salvation provides (John 3:3; Ephesians 4:1; Philippians 1:27). We can know that we are walking in the Spirit if our lives are showing forth the fruit of the Spirit which is love, joy, peace, patience, kindness, goodness, faithfulness, gentleness, and self-control (Galatians 5:22,23). Being filled (walking) with the Spirit is the same as allowing the word of Christ (the Bible) to richly dwell in us

(Colossians 3:16).

The result is thankfulness, singing, and joy (Ephesians 5:18-20; Colossians 3:16). Children of God will be led by the Spirit of God (Romans 8:14). When Christians choose not to walk in the Spirit, thereby sinning and grieving Him, provision has been made for restoration through confession of the wrongdoing (Ephesians 4:30; 1 John 1:9). To "walk in the Spirit" is to follow the Spirit's leading. It is essentially to "walk with" the Spirit, allowing Him to guide your steps and conform your mind. To summarize, just as we have received Christ by faith, by faith He asks us to walk in Him, until we are taken to heaven and will hear from the Master, "Well done!" (Colossians 2:5; Matthew 25:23).

Recommended Resource: The Wonderful Spirit-Filled Life by Charles Stanley

Romans 8 are a good chapter to meditate on to learn to walk in the Spirit."There is therefore now no condemnation to those who are in Christ Jesus, who do not walk according to the flesh, but according to the Spirit. For the law of the Spirit of life in Christ Jesus has made me free from the law of sin and death. For what the law could not do in that it was weak through the flesh, God did by sending His own Son in the likeness of sinful flesh, on account of sin: He condemned sin in the flesh, that the righteous requirement of the law might be fulfilled in us who do not walk according to the flesh but according to the Spirit. For those who live according to the flesh set their minds on the things of the flesh, but those who live according to the Spirit, the things of the Spirit. For to be carnally minded is death, but to be spiritually minded is life and peace. Because the carnal mind is enmity against God; for it is not subject to the law of God, nor indeed can be. So then, those who are in the flesh cannot please God. But you are not in the flesh but in the Spirit, if indeed the Spirit of God dwells in you. Now if anyone does not have the Spirit of Christ, he is not His. And if Christ is in you, the body is dead because of sin, but the Spirit is life because of righteousness. But if the Spirit of Him who raised Jesus from the dead dwells in you, He who raised Christ from the dead will also give life to your mortal bodies through His Spirit who dwells in you. Therefore, brethren, we are debtors—not to the flesh, to live according to the flesh. For if you live according to the flesh you will die; but if by the Spirit you put to death the deeds of the body, you will live. For as many as are led by the Spirit of God, these are sons of God. For you did not receive the spirit of bondage again to fear, but you received the Spirit of adoption by whom we cry out, "Abba, Father." The Spirit Himself bears witness with our spirit that we are children of God, and if children, then heirs—heirs of God and joint heirs with Christ, if indeed we suffer with Him, that we may also be glorified together. For I consider that the sufferings of this present time are not worthy to be compared with the glory which shall be revealed in us. For the earnest expectation of the creation eagerly waits for the revealing of the sons of God. For the creation was subjected to futility, not willingly, but because of Him who subjected it in hope; because the creation itself also will be delivered from the bondage of corruption into the glorious liberty of the children of God. For we know that the whole creation groans and labors with birth pangs together until now. Not only that, but we also who have the first fruits of the Spirit, even we ourselves groan within ourselves, eagerly waiting for the adoption, the redemption of our body. For we were saved in this hope, but hope that is seen is not hope; for why does one still hope for what he sees? But if we hope for what we do not see, we eagerly wait for it with perseverance. Likewise the Spirit also helps in our weaknesses. For we do not know what we should pray for as we ought, but the Spirit Himself makes intercession for us with groaning's which cannot be uttered. Now He who searches the hearts knows what the mind of the Spirit is, because He makes intercession for the saints according to the will of God. And we know that all things work together for good to those who love God, to those who are the called according to His purpose. For whom He foreknew, He also predestined to be conformed to the image of His Son, that He might be the firstborn among many brethren. Moreover whom He predestined, these He also called; whom He called, these He also justified; and whom He justified, and these He also glorified. What then shall we say to these things? If God is for us, who can be against us? He who did not spare His own Son, but delivered Him up for us all, how shall He not with Him also freely give us all things? Who shall bring a charge against God's elect? It is God who justifies. Who is he who condemns? It is Christ who died, and furthermore is also risen, who is even at the right hand of God, who also makes intercession for us. Who shall separate us from the love of Christ? Shall tribulation, or distress, or persecution, or famine, or nakedness, or peril, or sword? As it is written:

"For Your sake we are killed all day long;

We are accounted as sheep for the slaughter." Yet in all these things we are more than conquerors through Him who loved us. For I am persuaded that neither death nor life, nor angels nor principalities nor powers, nor things present nor things to come, nor height nor depth, nor any other created thing, shall be able to separate us from the love of God which is in Christ Jesus our Lord."

Romans 8:1-39

Father God I ask that you help me live life from a heavenly perspective rather than an earthly perspective. We are living in the end times and this very well may be the last generation that will not see death. Even if it is not, this is the last generation for some of you reading this book. We have lived a half century or more and some of us are ready to depart. I pray that before you depart that you will build up your rewards in heaven by building up those people within your sphere of influence. God is into people more than buildings and programs.

EPILOGUE

This book is about finding our value in life. Through this journey we call life we engage our life with multitudes of people. People influence us and we influence them. Let us not except the negativity from others but let us influence others and give people value. How many people do we influence? The answer is limitless. You could only influence one person in your life, but maybe that one person would go on to cure cancer, or become a Nobel Prize winner for inventing a replacement to gasoline, or become President of the US - and so how many people would you say that you influenced? Everyone is precious and worthy of value and respect - and if we all remember that each one of our interactions with people could someday result in a magnificent turn of events, we could positively influence so many people, and change the world.

BIO

William carries the anointing of a prophet and psalmist. He is also a Bible teacher, author and international speaker. He operates in all of the Spiritual gifts. He uses the gifts as the Holy Spirit wills. One of William's great desires is to lead others to Christ and to follow Holy Spirit wherever He leads.

www.ingramcontent.com/pod-product-compliance
Lightning Source LLC
Chambersburg PA
CBHW051042030426
42339CB00006B/157

* 9 7 8 1 7 7 5 0 3 3 0 2 8 *